WRITE IT YOUR WAY

DOVER PUBLICATIONS, INC.
MINEOLA, NEW YORK

D1510843

Bibliographical Note

Write It Your Way, first published by Dover Publications, Inc., in 2015, contains pages from the following online workbooks published by Education.com: *Reading Like a Writer, Writing Like a Reader; Journal Prompts For Kids; Opinion Writing;* and *Heroes and Villains: Story Writing.*

International Standard Book Number

ISBN-13: 978-0-486-80270-1
ISBN-10: 0-486-80270-1

Manufactured in the United States by Courier Corporation
80270101   2015
www.doverpublications.com

CONTENTS

CONTENTS

READING LIKE A WRITER, WRITING LIKE A READER

Talking About Literature

Learning these literary terms will come in handy as you complete the worksheets in this book.

ACTION
The events that take place in a literary work.

AUTOBIOGRAPHY
The story of a person's life told by him- or herself. It is always written in the first person.

BIOGRAPHY
The true story of a person's life that is told by another person. It is always written in the third person.

CHARACTER
A person or non-human, in the story.

CONFLICT
The struggle between two forces. The conflict often provides the main ACTION and spotlights the literary PLOT.

FANTASY
FICTION that uses magic or other supernatural elements.

FICTION
Literary works in which the characters and the plot are all made up.

Talking About Literature

Learning these literary terms will come in handy as you complete the worksheets in this book.

GENRE
The type of writing a book uses, such as FICTION, NONFICTION, SCIENCE FICTION, FANTASY, BIOGRAPHY, etc.

IMAGERY
The use of images, descriptions or figures of speech like METAPHORS and SIMILES to help the reader visualize a mood, concept, or CHARACTER.

INTERPRETATION
The ideas or explanations a reader has about the literary work's meaning.

IRONY
A technique in which a character or plot device is not as it would seem.

METAPHOR
A figure of speech that says one thing is another, revealing similar qualities in the two things. Example: *His voice was a soft wind that lulled me to sleep.*

MOOD
The atmosphere in a literary work, meant to evoke certain feelings from a reader.

NARRATOR
The speaker in a literary work.

NONFICTION
The opposite of FICTION. Any piece of writing that presents the truth about people and events.

PLOT
The literary work's ACTION, or events that move the story along.

Talking About Literature

Learning these literary terms will come in handy as you complete the worksheets in this book.

POINT OF VIEW
The perspective of the story's NARRATOR. There are three different classifications:
1) First Person
Speaker uses the pronoun "I."
2) Second Person
Speaker uses the pronoun "You."
3) Third Person
Speaker uses the pronoun(s) "He," "She," "It," or "They."

PROTAGONIST & ANTAGONIST
The protagonist is the central character in a literary work. The antagonist is an important character who often is in conflict with the protagonist.

SCIENCE FICTION
FICTION that includes scientific discoveries or technologies that we don't have in the present.

SETTING
The time and place in which the literary work's ACTION takes place.

SIMILE
A kind of METAPHOR that is introduced using the words "as," "as if," or "like."
Example: His voice sounded like a soft wind.

SYMBOL (SYMBOLISM)
Something that represents or stands for another thing.

THEME
The meaning or general ideas expressed in a work of literature.

TONE
The author's attitude towards the story and/or the story's readers.

Crossword Puzzle

Across

1. The atmosphere in a literary work, meant to evoke certain feelings from a reader.
2. When a protagonist struggles to get what he wants, this is called _____.
5. *Harry Potter* is an example of a _____ book.
6. The speaker in a literary work.
9. "My love is like a red, red, rose" is an example of a_____.
10. A technique in which a character or plot device is not as it would actually seem.
11. The type of writing, such as fiction or nonfiction.
13. "The sweet smell of orange blossoms reminded her of home" is called _____.
14. The literary work's action, as well as all other circumstances that move the story along.
16. A person, human or non-human in the story.
17. Greg Heffley is the _____ of The *Diary of a Wimpy Kid*.
18. Star Wars is an example of _____.
19. "A long time ago in a galaxy far, far away" is a sentence that gives the _____ of the story.

Down

1. "Your love is my sunshine" is an example of a_____.
3. Something that represents or stands for another thing.
4. *The Diary of Anne Frank* is an example of a _____ book.
7. The author's attitude towards the story and/or the story's readers.
8. The meaning or general ideas expressed in a work of literature.
12. The Big Bad Wolf is the _____ of *Little Red Riding Hood*.
15. The events that take place in a literary work.

5

 # It's All About CONFLICT

Most plots depend on conflict. How a character handles a particular problem will drive the action. Here are some different kinds of conflict:

Individual vs. Individual

This conflict is typically between an individual person and another person. It can also be between groups of people.

Individual vs. Society

This conflict occurs when characters go against a set of rules. It can also occur when characters break from "normal" behavior by doing something that might shock or offend polite society.

Individual vs. Technology

This happens when a character is in conflict with a kind of technology that threatens them. Lots of science fiction stories have this kind of conflict.

Individual vs. Nature

This happens when characters are thrown into the wild and must fend for themselves. Will they find food? Shelter? Can they protect themselves against wild animals and other dangers?

Individual vs. Self

This happens when characters are in conflict with something about themselves. They may be facing a problem like self-esteem or trying to control their temper.

Identify the CONFLICT

Match the story summaries below with the conflict that you think fits best. (Some may have more than one answer.)

1. A young Jewish girl hides from the Nazis in an attic in Holland. _____

2. In the future, a family lives in a smart house that does everything for them. It even has a room where anything they imagine will appear. One day the children imagine an African veldt with wild animals that threatens their parents. _____

3. A man walking on a trail in the Yukon on a very cold day gets very wet. He can't stay warm and tries to build a fire. When the fire goes out he tries to run to keep warm; even running doesn't warm him._____

4. A boy who is jealous of the new boy in town also desperately wants his approval. He does something risky in order to impress him. _____

Find the Clues

What Genre Is This?

Authors don't always tell you what genre their books are, but they do give you clues. Read the passage below and see if you can use clues to tell what the genre is.

Either the well was very deep, or she fell very slowly, for she had plenty of time as she went down to look about her and to wonder what was going to happen next. First, she tried to look down and make out what she was coming to, but it was too dark to see anything; then she looked at the sides of the well, and noticed that they were filled with cupboards and book-shelves; here and there she saw maps and pictures hung upon pegs. She took down a jar from one of the shelves as she passed; it was labeled 'ORANGE MARMALADE', but to her great disappointment it was empty: she did not like to drop the jar for fear of killing somebody, so managed to put it into one of the cupboards as she fell past it.

'Well!' thought _____ to herself, 'after such a fall as this, I shall think nothing of tumbling down stairs! How brave they'll all think me at home! Why, I wouldn't say anything about it, even if I fell off the top of the house!' (Which was very likely true.)

Down, down, down. Would the fall NEVER come to an end! 'I wonder how many miles I've fallen by this time?' she said aloud.

1. Do you think this passage is from a work of fiction or nonfiction? **A.** Fiction **B.** Nonfiction

1a. Write a complete sentence that explains why the passage is fiction or nonfiction.

_____

1b. Underline the clues in the text that helped you decide.

2. Do you think this passage is from a work of fantasy or science fiction? **A.** Fantasy **B.** Science Fiction

2a. Write a complete sentence that explains why the passage is fantasy or science fiction.

_____

2b. Underline the clues in the text that helped you decide.

Find the Clues
Character Profile

Getting to know characters, whether they're fictional or real, is one of the things that makes reading interesting. We can learn a lot about characters just from small details. Look for the clues in the following passages and see what information you can pick up. How many answers on the character profile can you provide?

When she opened her eyes in the morning it was because a young housemaid had come into her room to light the fire and was kneeling on the hearth-rug raking out the cinders noisily. Mary lay and watched her for a few moments and then began to look about the room. She had never seen a room at all like it and thought it curious and gloomy. The walls were covered with tapestry with a forest scene embroidered on it. There were fantastically dressed people under the trees and in the distance there was a glimpse of the turrets of a castle. There were hunters and horses and dogs and ladies. Mary felt as if she were in the forest with them. Out of a deep window she could see a great climbing stretch of land which seemed to have no trees on it, and to look rather like an endless, dull, purplish sea.

"What's that?" she said, pointing out of the window.

Martha, the young housemaid, who had just risen to her feet, looked and pointed also.

"That there?" she said.

"Yes."

"That's th' moor," with a good-natured grin. "Does tha' like it?"

"No," answered Mary. "I hate it."

"That's because tha'rt not used to it," Martha said, going back to her hearth. "Tha' thinks it's too big an' bare now. But tha' will like it."

"Do you?" inquired Mary.

"Aye, that I do," answered Martha, cheerfully polishing away at the grate. "I just love it. It's none bare. It's covered wi' growin' things as smells sweet. It's fair lovely in spring an' summer when th' gorse an' broom an' heather's in flower. It smells o' honey an' there's such a lot o' fresh air — an' th' sky looks so high an' th' bees an' skylarks makes such a nice noise hummin' an' singin'. Eh! I wouldn't live away from th' moor for anythin'".

Character Profile

Name:_____

Gender (male/female): _____

Age: _____

Birthplace: _____

Physical features (what does the character look like): _____

_____

Type of home/ neighborhood: _____

_____

Time in history: _____

Brothers and sisters: _____

Mother and father and their occupations: _____

Friends: _____

Enemies: _____

Other important people: _____

Likes and interests: _____

What bores or annoys the character?: _____

Attitude toward work or school: _____

Strongest positive personality trait:_____

Strongest negative personality trait: _____

Situation or problem the character is facing: _____

_____

Find the Clues

Character Profile

Use the same instructions and character profile for this worksheet.

Alice was beginning to get very tired of sitting by her sister on the bank, and of having nothing to do: once or twice she had peeped into the book her sister was reading, but it had no pictures or conversations in it, 'and what is the use of a book,' thought Alice 'without pictures or conversation?' So she was considering in her own mind (as well as she could, for the hot day made her feel very sleepy and stupid), whether the pleasure of making a daisy-chain would be worth the trouble of getting up and picking the daisies, when suddenly a White Rabbit with pink eyes ran close by her. There was nothing so VERY remarkable in that; nor did Alice think it so VERY much out of the way to hear the Rabbit say to itself, 'Oh dear! Oh dear! I shall be late!' (when she thought it over afterwards, it occurred to her that she ought to have wondered at this, but at the time it all seemed quite natural); but when the Rabbit actually TOOK A WATCH OUT OF ITS WAISTCOAT-POCKET, and looked at it, and then hurried on, Alice started to her feet, for it flashed across her mind that she had never before seen a rabbit with either a waistcoat-pocket, or a watch to take out of it, and burning with curiosity, she ran across the field after it, and fortunately was just in time to see it pop down a large rabbit-hole under the hedge.

Character Profile

Name:_____

Gender (male/female): _____

Age: _____

Birthplace: _____

Physical features (what does the character look like): _____
_____

Type of home/ neighborhood: _____
_____

Time in history: _____

Brothers and sisters: _____

Mother and father and their occupations: _____

Friends: _____

Enemies: _____

Other important people: _____

Likes and interests: _____

What bores or annoys the character?: _____

Attitude toward work or school: _____

Strongest positive personality trait:_____

Strongest negative personality trait: _____

Situation or problem the character is facing: _____
_____

Comparing Characters
Mary & Alice

In the passages below, Mary Lennox from *The Secret Garden*, by Frances Hodgson Burnett and Alice from *Alice's Adventures in Wonderland*, by Lewis Carroll, are two young girls who both find themselves in strange new places. Read the passages below and compare how they respond to their new surroundings.

The Secret Garden

On and on they drove through the darkness, and though the rain stopped, the wind rushed by and whistled and made strange sounds. The road went up and down, and several times the carriage passed over a little bridge beneath which water rushed very fast with a great deal of noise. Mary felt as if the drive would never come to an end and that the wide, bleak moor was a wide expanse of black ocean through which she was passing on a strip of dry land.

"I don't like it," she said to herself. "I don't like it," and she pinched her thin lips more tightly together.

Alice's Adventures in Wonderland

Either the well was very deep, or she fell very slowly, for she had plenty of time as she went down to look about her and to wonder what was going to happen next. First, she tried to look down and make out what she was coming to, but it was too dark to see anything; then she looked at the sides of the well, and noticed that they were filled with cupboards and book-shelves; here and there she saw maps and pictures hung upon pegs. She took down a jar from one of the shelves as she passed; it was labeled 'ORANGE MARMALADE', but to her great disappointment it was empty: she did not like to drop the jar for fear of killing somebody, so managed to put it into one of the cupboards as she fell past it.

"Well!" thought _____ to herself, "after such a fall as this, I shall think nothing of tumbling down stairs! How brave they'll all think me at home! Why, I wouldn't say anything about it, even if I fell off the top of the house!" (Which was very likely true.)

Down, down, down. Would the fall NEVER come to an end! "I wonder how many miles I've fallen by this time?" she said aloud.

Comparing Characters
Mary & Alice

Use the chart below to record any similarities or differences in the way Mary and Alice respond to the places they are entering. You might not have an answer for each box in the chart.

	Similarities	Differences
Places		
Character's thoughts and attitudes. Are they positive or negative?		
Characters' actions. Even very small actions are important.		

Look at the chart. How are Mary and Alice different from one another? Fill in the blanks to create a comparison.

Even though Mary and Alice both _____,

they are very different people. When Mary finds herself in a _____ place she

_____, whereas when Alice finds herself in a

_____ place _____.

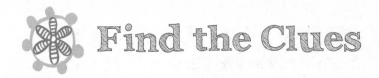

Find the Clues

Authors don't always tell you exactly where the setting is. Instead, they might give you lots of clues. See if you can find the clues in this passage that tell you what the setting is.

> On and on they drove through the darkness, and though the rain stopped, the wind rushed by and whistled and made strange sounds. The road went up and down, and several times the carriage passed over a little bridge beneath which water rushed very fast with a great deal of noise. Mary felt as if the drive would never come to an end and that the wide, bleak moor was a wide expanse of black ocean through which she was passing on a strip of dry land.

Quiz Questions

1. The main character, Mary, is sitting inside a _____ that is

(stopped or moving) _____ .

1a. Underline the clues in red.

2. What time of day is it? A. Middle of the day   B. Early morning   C. Nighttime

2a. Underline the clues in blue.

3. How would you describe the weather conditions? _____

3a. Underline the clues in yellow.

4. Do you think the author wants readers to think of this setting as a scary place or a safe

place for Mary? _____

4a. Underline the words or phrases that support your answer in green.

5. Find the metaphor! In this passage the author compares the moor to something else. What is it?

_____

Draw a picture below to illustrate the setting.

Write Your Own Setting
Part One: Create a Setting

Now, you try: Create your own setting for a story without naming where it is. You will plant clues in the text later.

1. Choose a Place: Mountains, ocean, house, neighborhood, forest, jungle, another galaxy, etc. (These are just some suggestions.)

Write your choice here:

_____

2. Choose a Time of Day: Dawn, afternoon, dinnertime, middle of the night, sunset...any others you can think of.

Write your choice here:

_____

3. Choose a Feeling: mysterious, scary, peaceful, exciting, fun, sad, stressful, romantic, adventurous.

Write your choice here:

4. Choose a Simple Action: driving, walking, eating dinner, doing homework, reading, watching tv, running away from something, talking to someone....

Write your choice here:

_____

Sight

Write down as many words you can think of that describe what someone would be seeing in your setting.

_____

_____

_____

Sound

What sounds might someone hear? Write as many as you can think of.

_____

_____

_____

Feeling or Touch

These aren't feelings inside of you, but are physical feelings such as cold, wet, soft, etc.

_____

_____

_____

Taste

_____

_____

_____

Move on to the next worksheet and write up your setting.

Write Your Own Setting
Setting Clues Using the Five Senses

Authors use sensory details to help them communicate information about setting and character. Brainstorm some sensory words about the setting you created.

Here is an example with sensory words in **bold**:

> *My shoes were* **squeaking loudly** *as I walked. I kept my eyes on the* **shiny wood** *floor, watching each step my feet were making, until I got to the microphone. It was* **cool to the touch** *-- very different from the general atmosphere, which was* **stuffy, airless,** *and* **uncomfortably warm.** **Sweat dripped down my back**. *I looked up and saw my classmates in rows that seemed to be* **stretching out forever**. *Their* **faces were a blur**.

Can you guess where this character is and what he is doing and feeling?

_____

_____

_____

_____

_____

Imagine yourself as a character in this setting, either as the speaker or a member of the audience. What would you be seeing, hearing, feeling, smelling, or even tasting? The words you come up with will be sensory words that you can use in your description on the next page.

_____

_____

_____

Write Your Own Dialogue

Dialogue is a conversation between two or more characters in a story.

Using one of the situations below, write dialogue between two speakers. Go back and forth so each speaker has at least 6 turns.

Situations

- Someone is telling his or her best friend that he or she will be moving away.
- A student is asking a teacher to let her (or him) turn in an assignment late.
- Two animals are talking about their owners.

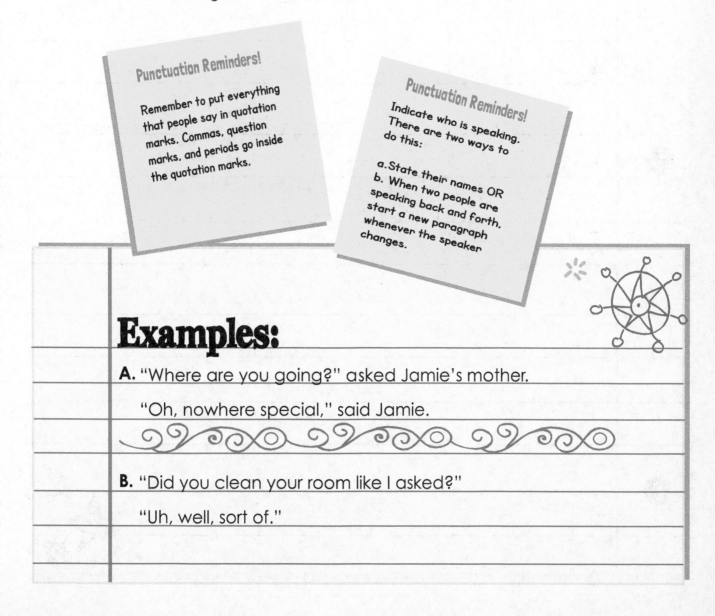

Punctuation Reminders!

Remember to put everything that people say in quotation marks. Commas, question marks, and periods go inside the quotation marks.

Punctuation Reminders!

Indicate who is speaking. There are two ways to do this:

a. State their names OR
b. When two people are speaking back and forth, start a new paragraph whenever the speaker changes.

Examples:

A. "Where are you going?" asked Jamie's mother.

"Oh, nowhere special," said Jamie.

B. "Did you clean your room like I asked?"

"Uh, well, sort of."

Write Your Own Dialogue

Now it's your turn to write your own dialogue. Use the previous page and reminders to help you.

Great job!

_____

is an Education.com writing superstar

JOURNAL PROMPTS
FOR KIDS

MENU

Name your sandwich

Draw what it looks like here

Create a new type of sandwich! It can involve any ingredients you like. Maybe it's a specialty sandwich you make all the time, or maybe it's something totally new. Be creative and have fun.

★ Ingredients

1	
2	
3	
4	
5	
6	
7	
8	
9	
10	

★ How to Make

CREATIVE WRITING

Invent a new animal! Your animal can be anything you want. It can have horns, a tail, teeth, gills, wings, claws, etc. It can be a hybrid, which means it's a mix of a few different animals. It can be a sea creature or a land creature. Draw a picture of your animal, and write about any special abilities it has.

NAME YOUR ANIMAL

DRAW YOUR ANIMAL HERE

HAVE FUN AND BE CREATIVE!

Create a comic book character!

What does your character look like?

Describe your character's normal life.

name of your character

What happens to the
character to drastically change his/her life?

Describe any special abilities your
character has.

Describe any sidekicks the character has.

Describe how the character came to get
those abilities.

Describe the character's arch-nemesis.

If you could have ONE superpower, what would it be? What would you do with your new power?

ZAP

MY SUPERPOWER

3 REASONS MY SUPERPOWER ROCKS

3 THINGS I WILL DO WITH MY SUPERPOWER

OVERALL, MY SUPERPOWER IS...

TAKE YOUR IDEAS AND WRITE A PARAGRAPH
ABOUT YOUR SUPERPOWER.

_____

_____

_____

_____

_____

_____

_____

_____

_____

_____

_____

_____

_____

_____

_____

_____

Who is your favorite fictional character? He or she could be from a movie, a book or a TV show. Imagine you got to spend a whole day with that character! What would you do? Where would you go? Write a story about your day together.

DRAW YOUR CHARACTER HERE!

Which season is your favorite, fall, winter, spring or summer? Why? Give three reasons why you enjoy that season more than the others. Then write down any supporting evidence and facts that you have to support your argument.

_____

_____

_____

_____

_____

_____

_____

_____

_____

_____

_____

You wake up in a different country. No one speaks your language, you don't know anyone, and you don't even know where you are! What do you do next?

你好

こんにちは

Pick one word to describe yourself. It can be any word—it doesn't have to be a descriptive word, it can be a noun or a verb. Write it down in the space provided. Then explain why you chose that word.

HELLO
If I could choose one word to describe myself, it would be...

Find the extraordinary in the ordinary! Write a poem about what you've done so far today. Even if it's not that exciting, find a way to make it so.

What is **ONE THING** that you love to do more than anything? It could be playing a sport, playing music, dancing, drawing, swimming, doing math, sleeping... Why do you like doing that thing? Do you think you could do that for a career? Write up your plan of action so that you are able to have a job doing the thing you love most.

REQUIREMENTS: Your plan must involve higher education or special training at some point, and your ultimate job must help the world in some way.

♥ ....
....
....
....
....
....
....
....
....
....
....
....
....
....

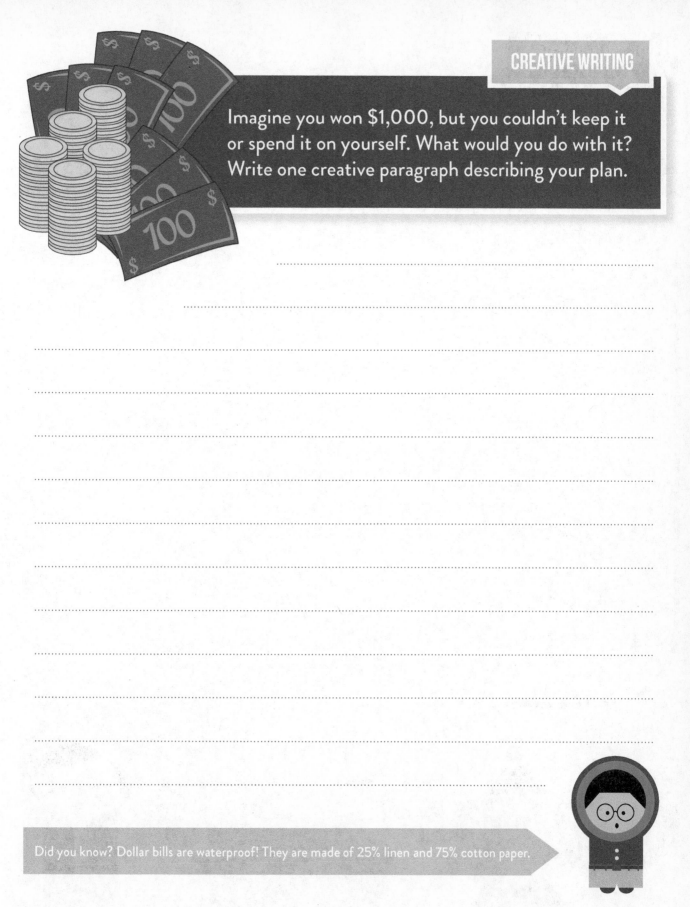

Imagine you won $1,000, but you couldn't keep it or spend it on yourself. What would you do with it? Write one creative paragraph describing your plan.

Did you know? Dollar bills are waterproof! They are made of 25% linen and 75% cotton paper.

A genie has granted you three wishes! There are some rules though—you can't wish for more wishes, you can't wish for money and you can't wish for anything bad to happen. What will your three wishes be and why?

Would you rather...
Travel through time, or travel through outer space?

....
....
....
....
....
....
....
....
....
....
....
....
....
....
....
....

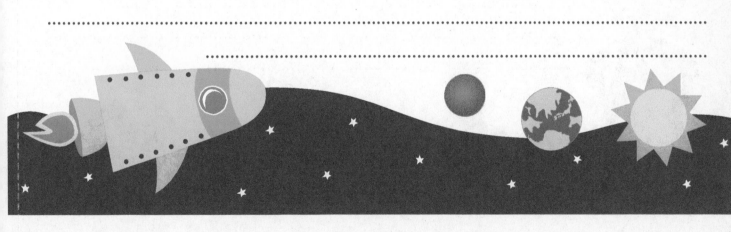

Would you rather...
Befriend an alien, or befriend a monster?

....

....

....

....

....

....

....

....

....

....

....

....

....

....

....

....

....

....

CREATIVE WRITING

Would you rather...
Discover gold, or discover a new species of animal?

Would you rather...
Be bitten by a vampire, or be bitten by a werewolf?

....

....

....

....

....

....

....

....

....

....

....

....

....

....

....

Would you rather...
Be haunted by a ghost, or be chased by a monster?

....
....
....
....
....
....
....
....
....
....
....
....

Haiku is a Japanese style of poetry that consists of three main components, although they are not necessarily required:

- Haiku has three lines, with the syllable pattern 5-7-5.
- Haiku poems are usually about a contrast between two items.
- Many haiku poems have a seasonal reference.

* Write a haiku about two random objects on your desk.

* Write a haiku about two pieces of clothing you are wearing today.

Haiku is a Japanese style of poetry that consists of three main components, although they are not necessarily required:

- Haiku has three lines, with the syllable pattern 5-7-5.
- Haiku poems are usually about a contrast between two items.
- Many haiku poems have a seasonal reference.

* Write a haiku about the weather today.

* Write a haiku about two of the four seasons.

CREATIVE
WRITING

Haiku is a Japanese style of poetry that consists of three main components, although they are not necessarily required:

- Haiku has three lines, with the syllable pattern 5-7-5.
- Haiku poems are usually about a contrast between two items.
- Many haiku poems have a seasonal reference.

* Write a haiku about your favorite TV show.

* Write a haiku about a famous person.

Great Job!

_____

is an Education.com writing superstar

OPINION WRITING

I. Support Identification

It's time to begin the process of understanding how to support your opinions with reasons and evidence. When writing a persuasive or opinionated essay, your opinions must be supported. The act of writing an opinion is not enough to make your opinion strong. It is very important to recognize supported statements versus unsupported statements, and to develop a sense of why the former works better in persuasive writing.

Here is a list of statements, half of which are opinions without support and half of which are opinions with support. You will identify each type of opinion below.

Some samples of **unsupported** opinions:

Cats are better than dogs. My cat Snowball chases flies in our kitchen. She looks so cute when she jumps from the table to the window sill.

Some samples of **supported** opinions:

Cats are better than dogs. They can leave the house by themselves and get exercise by jumping up on the roof and running around the neighborhood. They don't bark or make a lot of noise, so everyone gets enough sleep.

Now you try: Which opinion has supporting sentences and which opinion is unsupported? Write *supported* or *unsupported* for each example.

1. *Playing basketball is good exercise.* I am best at shooting the ball so my friends can't block it. My dribbling skills need to improve, and that's why I practice every day.

_____

2. *Playing basketball is good exercise.* You have to run a lot, and that's good for your heart and lungs. Shooting the ball builds hand-eye coordination, and jumping builds the leg muscles.

_____

II. Developing Support Statements

This three-part worksheet will help you develop the cognitive skills involved in moving from an opinion statement to a support statement.

Take a look at each statement in italics below. Then consider the question: "Why is this true?" This is the first step to start formulating better arguments. Each statement is an assumption, and needs some solid supporting evidence to back it up. Don't limit your supporting evidence to just your own ideas. Think about what other people might say to also support each of these statements of assumption.

Some sample opinion statements:
Watching a movie in a theater is better than watching a movie at home on TV.
Why is this true? Possible answer:

The screen and sound system are bigger, making for a more immersive experience.

People need to exercise more.
Why is this true? Possible answer:

Exercising keeps your body healthy.

Now you try:
1. Eating healthy is good for you.
Why is this true?

_____

2. Music puts me in a good mood.
Why is this true?

_____

3. Wearing sunblock prevents sunburns.
Why is this true?

_____

4. A dog is a much better pet than a fish.
Why is this true?

_____

5. I like to carry an umbrella when it rains.
Why is this true?

_____

III. Developing Support Statements

The word "support" in opinion writing doesn't only have to include your point of view. Consider what other people might think. Practice developing a strong list of reasons to support the statement, keeping your audience in mind. What might others say about the statement?

Step one: Think of your own reasons to support the statement.

Step two: Find more reasons and support by also thinking of reasons other people might have.

Brainstorm Use the steps above to give reasons to support these opinions:

1. Watching a movie in a theater is better than watching a movie at home on TV.

_____

_____

_____

2. Exercise is one of the most important ways you can take care of yourself.

_____

_____

_____

3. Being early is better than being late.

_____

_____

_____

IV. Developing Support Statements

Now it's time to combine what we've learned in Parts I, II, and III. Instead of supplying the topic statement that expresses the opinion, this worksheet asks you to choose the topic sentence, and provide two different support statements.

First, choose a topic. Then, write an opinion sentence about your topic. Next, you'll write down one reason why your opinion sentence is true. Finally, write a reason why someone else might think your opinion sentence is true. Now you have a complete, three-part opinion sequence!

Sample topics:

The best movie	Favorite animal
The best kind of ice cream	Dinner
Favorite holiday	Summer
Favorite show to watch on TV	Homework
Favorite book	Favorite sport to play

1. **TOPIC Sentence:**_____
Why is this true?

_____

Why would someone else say this was true?

_____

2. **TOPIC Sentence:**_____
Why is this true?

_____

Why would someone else say this was true?

_____

3. **TOPIC Sentence:**_____
Why is this true?

_____

Why would someone else say this was true?

_____

Writing for a Reader I

This worksheet is designed to help you begin to recognize how you can write with a certain reader, or audience, in mind. The ability to hold the concept of the reader in mind can be used for the process of idea generation; in other words, if you are asked to write for your mother, this information all by itself will generate support sentences that appeal to your mother alone. This isn't exactly tailoring writing, but it is one step on the road to being able to consider audience in opinion writing.

This worksheet is the first step in writing notes (or "memos") to people you know. The worksheet is not a prompt to write the note, just a planning step in the process of writing the note. The situtations below have two halves. Each half describes a situation for writing the note and the audience for it. Then you are asked to provide three reasons or points that will be included in the final note.

Sample situations:

A. You will be writing a note to your mother asking her if you can stay up one hour after your usual bedtime in order to see a certain TV show. What three reasons would you give her so that she will allow you to stay up?

_____

_____

_____

B. You will be writing a note to a good friend asking him or her to come over to your house after school to play. What three reasons would you give to convince him or her to come over to your house?

_____

_____

_____

Final Note:

_____

_____

_____

_____

_____

_____

_____

_____

Writing for a Reader II

This worksheet is a variant of "Writing for a Reader Worksheet I" with the same instructional goals. The worksheet has two halves. Each half describes a situation for writing the note and the audience for it. Then you are asked to provide three reasons or points that will be included in the final note, which you will write on the worksheet.

Sample situations:

A. You will be writing a note to a police officer asking him to come to your school and talk about his job. What three reasons would you give him so that he will come to your school?

_____

_____

_____

B. You will be writing a note to your favorite sports figure or musical artist asking her to send you an autographed picture. What three reasons would you give her so that she will send the picture?

_____

_____

_____

Final Note:

_____

_____

_____

_____

_____

_____

_____

_____

_____

_____

_____

_____

_____

_____

Writing for a Reader III

This worksheet is a variant of "Writing for a Reader Worksheet I" with the same instructional goals. The worksheet has two halves. Each half describes a situation for writing the note and the audience for it. Then you are asked to provide three reasons or points that will be included in the final note, which you will write on the worksheet.

Sample situations:

A. Write a note to your next-door neighbor, who has a mean dog that he lets roam around the neighborhood. What three reasons would you give so that he will keep his dog in his backyard?

_____

_____

B. Write a note to the mayor of your town or city asking her to fix the street light in front of your house that has been out for two months. What three reasons would you give her so that the light gets fixed?

_____

_____

Final Note:

_____

_____

_____

_____

_____

_____

_____

_____

_____

_____

_____

_____

_____

Change in Your Classroom

Is there a change you would like to see in your classroom?
As a student, you should be able to voice your opinion. If you give a clear statement of opinion and back it up with good evidence, or supporting statements, then your voice will be better heard and understood. Practice writing an opinion paragraph using the prompts shown below.

[?] What is one major *change* you would like to see in your classroom?

_____

_____

[?] Support #1:

_____

_____

[?] Support #2:

_____

_____

[?] Support #3:

_____

_____

[!] In conclusion,

_____

_____

_____

_____

Identifying Opinion SENTENCES

A statement of opinion is not narrative writing. In other words, it is not a story. An opinion is a person's own personal belief or point of view.

Read the list of sentences below, each of which belongs either in a piece of opinion writing or a piece of narrative writing. Identify each sentence as either opinion or narrative.

1. The dog ran into the street, followed by three kittens.

_____

2. People should be nicer to homeless people.

_____

3. After the car went through the red light, we heard the police siren.

_____

4. The bicycle lanes aren't big enough.

_____

5. When we jumped into the lake, we were not prepared for how cold the water was.

_____

6. Students need to be assigned more homework.

_____

Identifying:
Opinion
SENTENCES

A statement of opinion is not narrative writing. In other words, it is not a story. An opinion is a person's own personal belief or point of view.

Read the list of sentences below, each of which belongs either in a piece of opinion writing or a piece of narrative writing. Identify each sentence as opinion or narrative.

1. The elephant was scared by the mouse that entered his home.

_____

2. Toasted marshmallows are the best.

_____

3. When we sat next to the campfire, we did not expect it to be so hot!

_____

4. Hot chocolate is perfect for winter!

_____

5. The pool is way too cold.

_____

6. I always know when there is a football game by the loud cheers from the stadium.

_____

Identifying: Opinion SENTENCES

A statement of opinion is not narrative writing. In other words, it is not a story. An opinion is a person's own personal belief or point of view.

Read the list of sentences below, each of which belongs either in a piece of opinion writing or a piece of narrative writing.
Identify each sentence as opinion or narrative.

1. The newspaper is so boring to read.

_____

2. You could hear the music pound through the walls.

_____

3. The hardwood floors were cold on my bare feet.

_____

4. Playing video games is the best thing to do on a Saturday morning.

_____

5. Her hair was as yellow as the sun!

_____

6. After he finished his homework, he played basketball by the garage.

_____

Audience for Opinion Writing

To develop a general understanding of opinion writing, you need to get into the habit of thinking about your audience. Consider the different kinds of people you would write for in order to express an opinion.

Whether you're having a discussion with your parents, or deciding on an activity to do with friends, be sure to pay attention to your audience. Consider how you could modify your writing to please your audience.

1. Think about what goes on when you go to the movies with your family. Is there anything you'd like to change about movie night?

Your Audience: _____

Your Opinion: _____

_____

_____

2. What is good and what is bad about going to a county fair or a street fair? Is there anything you would like to change about the fair?

Your Audience: _____

Your Opinion: _____

_____

_____

PERSUASIVE PARAGRAPH WORKSHEET

LEARN TO SUPPORT YOUR OPINION

A persuasive paragraph states and supports an opinion. Follow the instructions below to write your own persuasive paragraph.

Use the subject below, then use this structure to write your paragraph:

SUBJECT: A new policy would ban Facebook access to all kids under the age of 18.

INTRODUCTION: State your position or opinion. Who is your audience? In other words, who are you trying to persuade? Keep your audience in mind when you write.

REASONS: List at least three reasons for your opinion. Think of your audience and what reasons might persuade them.

CONCLUSION: Restate your opinion in a way that relates it to a greater statement about the world or society.

INTRODUCTION: _____

_____

_____

REASON #1: _____

_____

_____

REASON #2: _____

_____

_____

REASON #3: _____

_____

_____

CONCLUSION: _____

_____

Opinion Paragraph Writing

Using what you learned and practiced in sections one and two, this worksheet first defines the characteristics of an opinion paragraph:

"A good opinion paragraph should have at least four sentences. The first sentence states your opinion, and the next three sentences give reasons why you have this opinion."

Read the sample prompts, and write in the spaces given.

Sample prompt:
Some students think teachers should assign more homework, and some students think teachers should assign less homework. What do you think?

Example opinion paragraph:
I think teachers should assign more homework. They should assign more homework because students need to learn more things. If students don't do homework, they watch too much TV. Plus, having more homework will give kids more responsibility.

1. Sample prompt:
Some people think that all kids should join a sport. What is your opinion on the subject?

_____

_____

_____

_____

_____

_____

_____

_____

_____

Opinion Paragraph Writing

2. *Sample prompt:*

Some students like taking P.E., and some students don't like it. What is your opinion about the Physical Education requirement in schools?

_____

_____

_____

_____

_____

_____

_____

_____

_____

_____

_____

_____

_____

_____

_____

Opinion Paragraph Writing

3. Sample prompt:

Some people think children should go to camp every summer, take classes, or spend the summer studying. Other people think children should just be allowed to stay at home and play. What do you think?

_____

_____

_____

_____

_____

_____

_____

_____

_____

_____

_____

_____

_____

_____

_____

_____

_____

Write a Letter to the Editor

Use Your Voice

Everyone has a voice in their community. Use yours by writing a letter to the editor of your local newspaper. This is a chance for you to voice your opinion about a community issue that is important to you.

Brainstorming Ideas

Think of an important public issue that affects your everyday life. Do you agree or disagree with it? How would you change things? Choose from the list below or come up with your own ideas.

- Dress codes in public schools
- Kids owning their own cell phones
- The most recent elections for your local government
- The voting age (18 years old)
- Find a news report or article that you agree or disagree with

- _____
- _____
- _____
- _____
- _____
- _____
- _____

Write a Letter to the Editor

My Local Newspaper: _____

Editor in Chief: _____

My Headline: _____

Date:_____

Dear Editor,

I am writing because _____

_____

_____

I feel very strongly about this because _____

_____

_____

_____

_____

I would like it if _____

_____

_____

_____

Thank you,

_____

Great job!

is an Education.com writing superstar

HEROES AND VILLAINS:
STORY WRITING

Eight of the finest superheroes and villains have gone missing! Their disappearance has caused a catastrophe at EPIC headquarters. Heroes and villains all over the world are starting to get restless. Time is running out! It is your mission to get to know these eight supers, track them down and find out why they went missing. Then, bring them home.

MISSING!

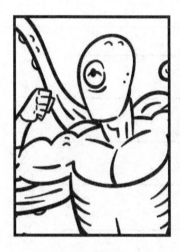

Captain
Kraken

Prospector
on Mars

Awful
Epoxy

Lucha
Libre

Molten
Martian

Bushido

Evil Genie

Celestial

AWFUL EPOXY

Don't run afoul of the Awful Epoxy, or you just might find yourself in a –dare we say it?– sticky situation. Was this mighty monster once a man, or has he always been this awful? Write his origin story.

_____

_____

_____

_____

_____

_____

_____

_____

_____

_____

LUCHA LIBRE

From the streets of Oaxaca comes Lucha Libre!, the only known luchador with superpowers. What do you think—is it legal to use your super-strength during a wrestling match? Write about his run-ins outside of the wrestling ring, and in it.

_____

_____

_____

_____

_____

_____

_____

_____

_____

_____

_____

BUSHIDO

Bushido is a super-samurai, trained to be the biggest, baddest warrior in the Japanese army. What are some of his special tactics? Give this noble warrior a backstory.

_____

_____

_____

_____

_____

_____

_____

_____

_____

_____

_____

_____

CAPTAIN KRAKEN

Even the uncharted depths of the sea cannot contain Captain Kraken, one of the most loathsome villains to rule the deep. How did he develop his terrifying tentacles? Make up an origin story for him.

_____

_____

_____

_____

_____

_____

_____

_____

_____

_____

MOLTEN MARTIAN

The Molten Martian isn't a bad guy, he just looks like one. What do you think: is he safe to come in contact with? Write about what his skin looks, feels, or even smells like.

_____

_____

_____

_____

_____

_____

_____

_____

_____

_____

_____

PROSPECTOR ON MARS

As a society, we've always dreamed of colonizing Mars. The Prospector already has. Now he's mining Mars for its natural resources.
What is his daily life like in this uninhabited territory?
Write a story about his tangles with natives, vigilantes and claim-jumpers.

_____

_____

_____

_____

_____

_____

_____

_____

_____

_____

CELESTIAL

No one knows much about the secretive Celestial. He spends his days roaming the heavens in his obscuring helmet, carrying his mighty spear. What do you think: is he good or evil? Write your opinion and make sure to back it up using facts about his past.

_____

_____

_____

_____

_____

_____

_____

_____

_____

_____

_____

EVIL GENIE

This genie doesn't grant wishes, so don't bother asking. He uses his powers to wreak havoc on unsuspecting humans. Which hero do you think is best suited to stop him? Write a story about who might be able to defeat him.

_____

_____

_____

_____

_____

_____

_____

_____

_____

_____

_____

CONGRATULATIONS!

You've finally caught up to the superheroes and villains. Now it's time to do some surveillance work. Use the blank comic strips below to show what you've been observing about our rogue supers.

FIGHT SCENE BETWEEN TWO OF THE CHARACTERS

DIALOGUE BETWEEN TWO
OF THE CHARACTERS

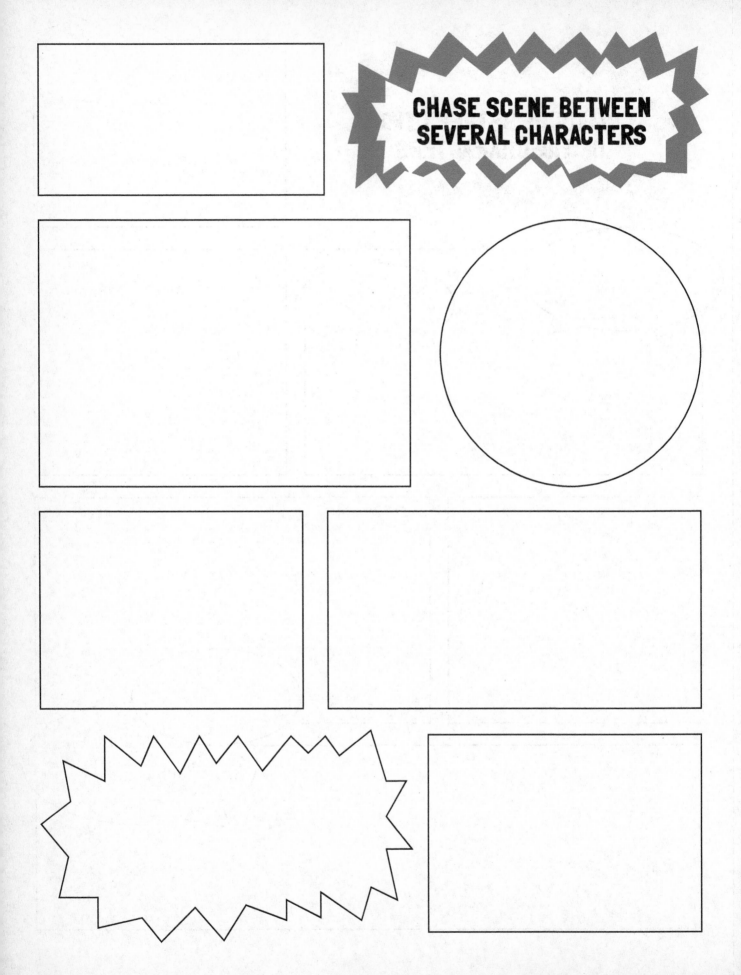

CHASE SCENE BETWEEN
SEVERAL CHARACTERS

INNER MONOLOGUE OF ONE OF THE CHARACTERS

HOLLYWOOD CAMERA 1

You've done such a great job on this case it looks like Hollywood is after your story! They want to make a movie out of the investigation you've been carrying out. It will star you and the eight supers you've been tracking. You're so excited that you decide to create a movie poster.

Have you ever noticed that, along with an image, movie posters usually include the title of the movie, a catchy tagline, and a list of the leading actors and the director? For your poster you'll even be including a synopsis of what the movie's story should be.

_____

TITLE OF THE MOVIE

_____

TAGLINE OF THE MOVIE

_____

_____

CAST   **DIRECTOR**

MAIN CHARACTERS

SETTING

PROBLEM OF THE STORY

A STORY EVENT

HOW THE PROBLEM IS SOLVED

THE ENDING

_____

_____

_____

_____

_____

_____

_____

_____

_____

_____

SYNOPSIS / PLOT

⭐ HERE'S AN EXAMPLE OF A MOVIE SYNOPSIS:

This summer, follow 14-year-old genius Kyle Smarte as he finds out summer camp means more than hikes and arts and crafts. He's out to take over the world super-genius style, but how will he do that when he can't even get an eye splice knot down pat? His parents sent him here, and while he avoids making friends as much as possible and builds up his plans for world domination, at summer camp meeting people is unavoidable. The story climaxes when Kyle and another kid get separated from the group during "the big hike" and have to work together to make it. By the end of the story, Kyle has had his life saved at least once, has saved others, and has found himself faced with real trouble. Turned out this super genius might actually be a superhero.

You've been noticing some interesting relationships forming among the eight rogue superheroes and villains. Explain how these characters are all connected.

EVIL GENIE — **BUSHIDO**

Differences

Similarities

Differences

HOW DO THEY KNOW EACH OTHER?

PROSPECTOR ON MARS

CAPTAIN KRAKEN

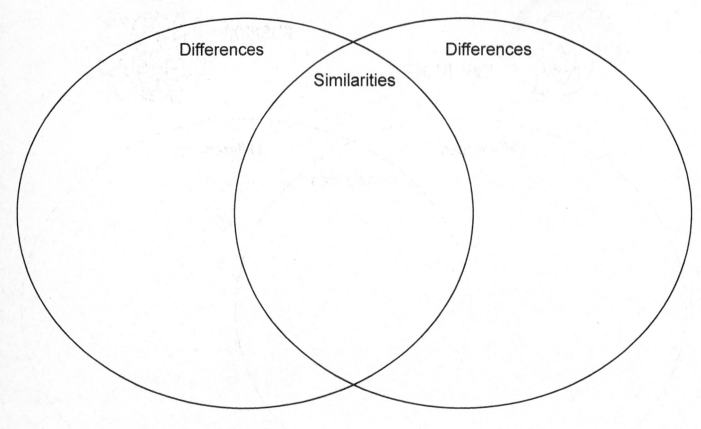

Differences

Differences

Similarities

HOW DO THEY KNOW EACH OTHER?

AWFUL EPOXY

MOLTEN MARTIAN

Differences   Similarities   Differences

HOW DO THEY KNOW EACH OTHER?

LUCHA LIBRE

CELESTIAL

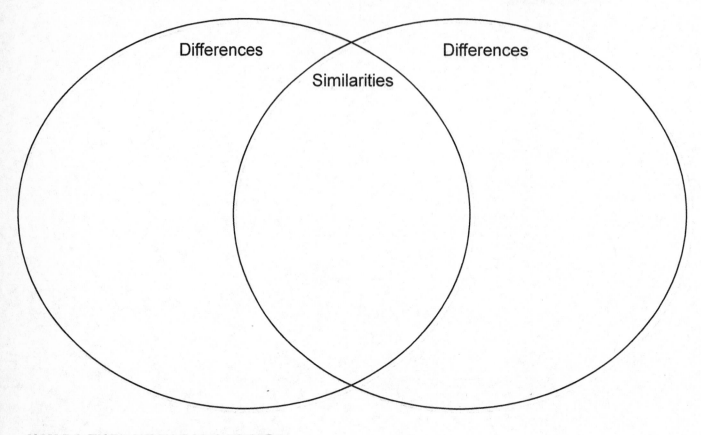

Differences

Similarities

Differences

HOW DO THEY KNOW EACH OTHER?

There has suddenly been a huge break in the case! It looks like your eight "missing" superheroes and villains have actually banded together on a super-top-secret mission to stop a super villain! He's never been seen before, but you caught a glimpse during your surveillance.

DRAW A PICTURE OF HIM HERE...

EXPLAIN 5 OF HIS PHYSICAL CHARACTERISTICS

_____

_____

_____

_____

_____

_____

EXPLAIN 5 OF HIS PERSONAL TRAITS

_____

_____

_____

_____

_____

_____

EXPLAIN HIS PLOT TO TAKE OVER THE WORLD!

WHAT IS HIS PLOT?

_____

_____

WHO IS HE?

_____

_____

HOW WILL HE TAKE OVER THE WORLD?

_____

_____

WHY WILL HE TAKE OVER THE WORLD?

_____

_____

WHEN WILL HE TAKE OVER THE WORLD?

_____

_____

CONGRATULATIONS! YOU'VE SOLVED THE CASE. NOW IT'S TIME FOR A DEBRIEFING. WE KNOW THAT YOU AND ALL OF THE CHARACTERS, INCLUDING THE SUPER-SUPER VILLAIN, HAD A BIG SHOWDOWN IN A BUSY DOWNTOWN AREA. USE THE LINES AND EMPTY BOXES BELOW TO FILL IN THE DETAILS AND DRAW PICTURES OF WHAT YOU SAW.

Great job!

is an Education.com writing superstar

ANSWERS

Crossword Puzzle

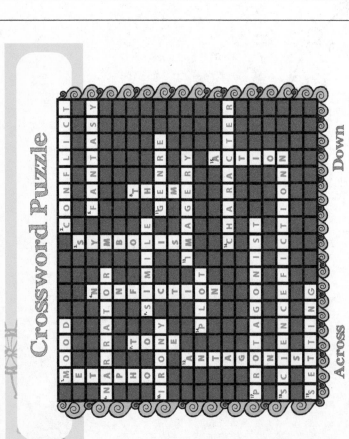

Across

1. The atmosphere in a literary work, meant to evoke certain feelings from a reader.
2. When a protagonist struggles to get what he wants this is called _____.
5. Harry Potter is an example of a _____ book.
6. The speaker in a literary work.
9. "My love is like a red, red, rose" is an example of a _____.
10. A technique in which a character or plot device is not as it would actually seem.
11. The type of writing, such as fiction or nonfiction.
13. "The sweet smell of orange blossoms reminded her of home" is called _____.
14. The literary work's action, as well as all other circumstances that move the story along.
16. A person, human or non-human in the story.
17. Greg Heffley is the _____ of The Diary of a Wimpy Kid.
18. Star Wars is an example of a _____.
19. "A long time ago in a galaxy far, far away" is a sentence that gives the _____ of the story.

Down

1. "Your love is my sunshine" is an example of a _____.
3. Something that represents or stands for another thing.
4. The Diary of Anne Frank is an example of a _____ book.
7. The author's attitude towards the story and/or the story's readers.
8. The meaning or general ideas expressed in a work of literature.
12. The Big Bad Wolf is the _____ of Little Red Riding Hood.
15. The events that take place in a literary work.

page 5

Identifying Opinion SENTENCES

A statement of opinion is not narrative writing. In other words, it is not a story. An opinion is a person's own personal belief or point of view.

Read the list of sentences below, each of which belongs either in a piece of opinion writing or a piece of narrative writing. Identify each sentence as either opinion or narrative.

1. The dog ran into the street, followed by three kittens.
narrative writing (fact)

2. People should be nicer to homeless people.
opinion writing (belief)

3. After the car went through the red light, we heard the police siren.
narrative writing (fact)

4. The bicycle lanes aren't big enough.
opinion writing (belief)

5. When we jumped into the lake, we were not prepared for how cold the water was.
narrative writing (fact)

6. Students need to be assigned more homework.
opinion writing (belief)

page 56

Opinion SENTENCES

A statement of opinion is not narrative writing. In other words, is not a story. An opinion is a person's own personal belief or point of view.

Read the list of sentences below, each of which belongs either in a piece of opinion writing or a piece of narrative writing. Identify each sentence as opinion or narrative.

1. The elephant was scared by the mouse that entered his home.
   narrative writing (fact)
2. Toasted marshmallows are the best.
   opinion writing (belief)
3. When we sat next to the campfire, we did not expect it to be so hot!
   narrative writing (fact)
4. Hot chocolate is perfect for winter!
   opinion writing (belief)
5. The pool is way too cold.
   opinion writing (belief)
6. I always know when there is a football game by the loud cheers from the stadium.
   narrative writing (fact)

Identifying: Opinion SENTENCES

A statement of opinion is not narrative writing. In other words, it is not a story. An opinion is a person's own personal belief or point of view.

Read the list of sentences below, each of which belongs either in a piece of opinion writing or a piece of narrative writing. Identify each sentence as opinion or narrative.

1. The newspaper is so boring to read.
   opinion writing (belief)
2. You could hear the music pound through the walls.
   narrative writing (fact)
3. The hardwood floors were cold on my bare feet.
   narrative writing (fact)
4. Playing video games is the best thing to do on a Saturday morning.
   opinion writing (belief)
5. Her hair was as yellow as the sun!
   narrative writing (fact)
6. After he finished his homework, he played basketball by the garage.
   narrative writing (fact)